D0515903

EASY ANSWERS

TO FIRST SCIENCE QUESTIONS ABOUT

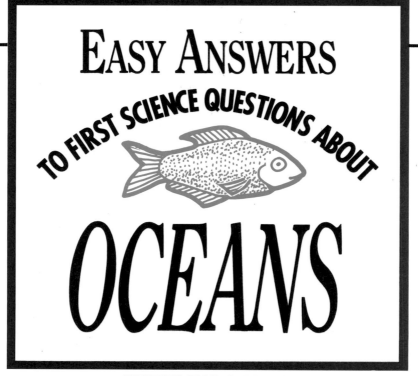

OCEANS

WRITTEN BY Q. L. PEARCE

ILLUSTRATED BY GIL HUNG

EXPERT CONSULTANTS: Rimmon C. Fay, Ph.D., Director, Pacific Bio-Marine Laboratories, Inglewood, California, and Ron Russo, author of *Pacific Coast Fish* and *Pacific Intertidal Life*

TO MARY AND JIM

An RGA Book

Copyright © 1991 by RGA Publishing Group, Inc.
This edition published in 1991 by SMITHMARK Publishers Inc.,
112 Madison Avenue, New York, NY 10016.
Manufactured in the United States of America.

ISBN 0-8317-2586-9

Q: HOW DEEP IS THE OCEAN?

Answer: The deepest point in all of Earth's oceans is in the Pacific Ocean, at a place called the Marianas Trench. One part of the trench is nearly seven miles below the surface. The land at the bottom of the ocean is as irregular as the dry land on which we live. There are valleys, canyons, wide flat plains, fiery volcanoes, and tall mountains. Some mountains in the ocean peek above the water's surface. These are islands.

Q: WHICH OCEAN IS THE LARGEST?

Answer: Earth's largest ocean is the Pacific Ocean. Covering more than 65 million square miles, this huge body of water is larger than the land area of all seven continents combined! It is about 11,000 miles across at its widest point. The waters of the Pacific Ocean touch the shores of five continents and more than 10,000 islands.

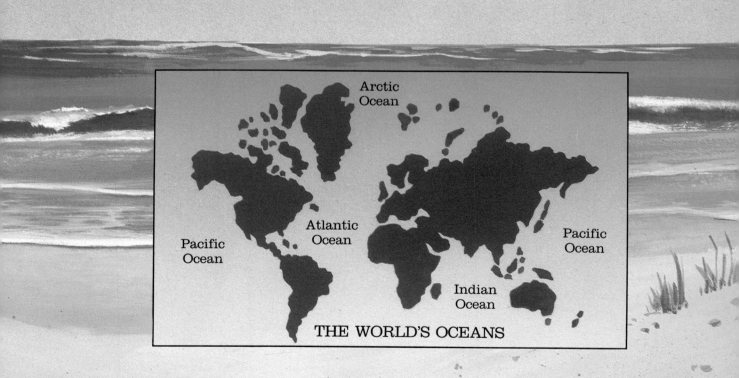

Arctic Ocean

Atlantic Ocean

Pacific Ocean

Pacific Ocean

Indian Ocean

THE WORLD'S OCEANS

Q: WHY IS THE OCEAN BLUE?

Answer: The ocean usually appears blue because of the way it absorbs and scatters sunlight. Water is made up of tiny particles called molecules, which are far too small for us to see. When light from the Sun passes through the water, it strikes these molecules. Some colors, such as red, are absorbed. Others, such as blue, are bounced back. Because more blue light is bounced back than any other color, we see the ocean as blue.

Q: DOES SUNLIGHT REACH THE BOTTOM OF THE OCEAN FLOOR?

Answer: No. The different colors in sunlight reach different depths, but no light reaches past a certain point. Red sea creatures appear to be brightly colored near the ocean's surface. At about thirty feet deep some fade to dull brown because the red light is absorbed by the water. Yellow is absorbed at about seventy-five feet. Between 100 and 300 feet deep, only blue light remains, so everything appears blue. Below 300 feet there is little or no light at all.

Q: HAVE THE OCEANS ALWAYS BEEN WHERE THEY ARE TODAY?

Answer: No. Many millions of years ago, when dinosaurs first roamed the Earth, the dry land was all part of one huge continent. The continent was surrounded by a single great ocean. Forces deep inside the planet caused the continent to break into several pieces, or plates. These splits were along lines called rift valleys. Seawater crept in to fill the gaps as the plates moved apart. Very slowly, the modern oceans were born.

MILLION YEARS AGO

TODAY

Q: HOW OLD IS THE OCEAN FLOOR?

Answer: Because the ocean floor is always being destroyed and renewed, no part of it is more than 200 million years old. From deep within the Earth, a steady flow of molten rock seeps up along the rift valleys and hardens into new ocean floor. The rock that forms the ocean floor is heavier than the rock that forms the continents. Where the sea meets dry land, ocean rock is often forced down beneath the land. Sinking deep into the Earth, it slowly becomes molten rock once again.

Q: WHAT IS SAND MADE OF?

Answer: Sand is made up mostly of tiny bits of rock. Along the seashore, rocks are worn away by the action of wind, waves, and other forces. Some rock particles from far inland are carried to the sea by rivers and rain. The tiny bits of rock, tumbled by waves and gusty winds, are ground down even smaller and finally become grains of sand. Heavier than water, the sand grains at last sink to the ocean floor or are deposited along the shore to form beaches.

Q: *IS THERE LIFE AT THE BOTTOM OF THE SEA?*

Answer: Yes. A variety of animals make their homes in the inky blackness of the deep ocean. Some fish, such as the anglerfish, have light-producing organs to attract their prey or mates in the darkness. In rift valleys far below the surface, areas called "hot vents" spew out very hot water. Near these vents there live some unusual animals—for example, six-foot-long, blood-red worms, each tucked inside its own white tube, and clams as large as Frisbees.

The glowing anglerfish

Q: *WHY IS THE OCEAN SALTY?*

Answer: Ocean water is salty because it contains certain minerals such as sodium chloride (common table salt). When the oceans first formed, they were made of fresh water. Over millions of years rain dissolved salts from rocks on land, and rivers and streams carried billions of tons of the salt to the oceans. The process still goes on today.

Q: DO WHALES DRINK SEAWATER?

Answer: Whales take in some seawater when they swallow a meal, but they don't rely on it as drinking water. Fish-eating whales (and dolphins) get water from their food. Another important source of water for whales is blubber, which is a layer of fat beneath the animal's skin. During periods when the whales do not feed, the blubber is burned by the whale to produce energy. One of the by-products of the fat is water.

Q: WHAT CAUSES THE TIDES?

Answer: Gravity causes the daily rise and fall of the sea level, known as the tide. The Moon's gravity tugs on Earth's ocean water, causing it to rise in a bulge. Two areas of water experience "high tide" at once: the area that faces the Moon and the area on the exact opposite side of Earth from the Moon. Areas in between experience "low tide." As Earth rotates, different points face the Moon, and the tide rises and falls accordingly. The Sun's gravity also affects the tides, but the influence of the Moon is much greater because it is much closer to Earth.

Q: WHAT IS A TIDE POOL?

Answer: A tide pool is a small body of water left behind at low tide. As the sea level lowers, rocks that are
normally under the waves are uncovered. Seawater is
often trapped in shallow pools between these rocks. A
tide pool is an ocean "oasis" for small creatures that
would otherwise be stranded on dry land. Creatures
that live in tide pools include spiny sea urchins and
starfish. The best time to see these animals is at low
"slack tide," which is about an hour before the low tide
begins to change to the high tide.

Q: WHAT IS A RIPTIDE?

Answer: A riptide is a fast-moving, offshore flow of water. Actually, it has nothing to do with the tides and is more properly called a rip current. A rip current develops when water brought inshore by waves builds up. The water finally drains through the oncoming waves and escapes back to sea as a narrow current. Rip currents can reach speeds of more than two miles per hour and can be dangerous to swimmers because the currents may carry them away from shore.

Riptide

Q: WHAT IS RED TIDE?

Answer: Red tide is caused by high numbers of very tiny, red sea organisms called dinoflagellates. When there are plenty of nutrients in the water and enough sunlight, billions of these plantlike organisms may suddenly "bloom" and cause the water to appear red. At night, however, they give breaking waves along the shore a *bluish* glow. The red tide can be deadly to fish because the organisms use up oxygen in the water. There can be as many as 60 million of them in one quart of seawater!

Q: WHERE DO SEASHELLS COME FROM?

Answer: Seashells are the coverings of certain animals such as scallops, oysters, clams, and sea snails. The shells are made mostly of minerals from the seawater and other materials produced by the animal. Most shells have three separate layers. The thin outer layer keeps the shell from dissolving in the seawater. The thick, hard middle layer protects the animal from harm. Finally, the smooth inner layer keeps the creature inside comfortable.

Q: WHY CAN YOU HEAR THE OCEAN IN A SEASHELL?

Answer: You cannot really hear the ocean in a seashell. The shape of a shell causes sound waves to break up, and what you hear when you place a shell to your ear is actually just jumbled sound waves. The jumbled sound waves sound much like the gentle lapping of ocean waves. The best shell to use to hear this sound is the shell of a large marine snail called a conch (KONK).

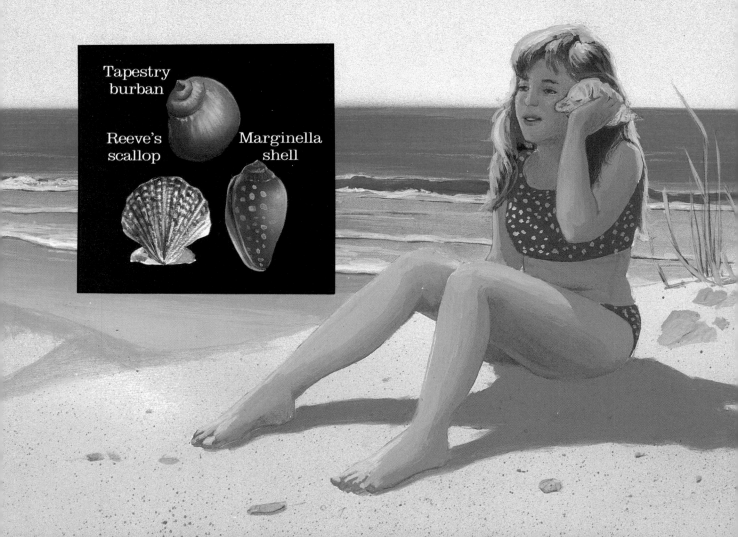

Tapestry burban

Reeve's scallop

Marginella shell

Q: *WHAT CAUSES WAVES?*

Answer: The wind causes most waves. A wave is a ridge of water on the surface of a body of water such as the ocean. The size of a wave depends on how fast, how long, and how far the wind blows. A wave can be a tiny ripple or a gigantic storm wave many feet tall. Huge waves called tsunamis (soo-NAM-eez) can rise to more than 100 feet high. These giant waves are caused not by the wind, but by earthquakes or volcanic eruptions.

Q: WHY DO WAVES BREAK ON THE SHORE?

Answer: Waves break on the shore because the deepest part of the wave begins to "feel" the bottom and slow down. As an incoming wave approaches the shore, it begins to drag on the shallow sea bottom. It becomes steep and top-heavy as water builds up behind it. The wave's top, or crest, moves faster than the rest of the wave and finally topples over with a foaming crash.

Q: WHY DO ICEBERGS FLOAT?

Answer: Icebergs float because they are lighter than the same amount of ocean water would be. Icebergs come from glaciers, which are huge, slow-moving "rivers" of ice that form on land from fresh water. When a glacier reaches the sea, large chunks break away from the forward edge and float away as icebergs. Only a small portion of an iceberg appears above the surface of the ocean. The rest of it is under water. Arctic icebergs can tower as much as 300 feet above the water.

Most of an iceberg
is beneath the water

Q: DOES THE ARCTIC OCEAN FREEZE COMPLETELY?

Answer: The Arctic Ocean never gets cold enough to freeze entirely. That's partly because of its salt content. However, the surface of the Arctic Ocean is covered with a crust of ice called the ice pack. Protected from the icy wind, the seawater under the ice pack remains liquid. The average depth of the ice pack is between eight and twelve feet, but in some places it extends down as far as 150 feet. Summer sunshine melts the surface of the ice and shrinks its borders, but it does not melt the ice completely.

Q: WHAT IS THE BIGGEST FISH?

Answer: The world's largest fish is the whale shark, which can weigh 12,000 pounds—as much as two African elephants! (Many whales are larger than that, but whales are mammals, not fish.) It isn't unusual for this huge creature to reach forty feet in length, and some whale sharks as long as sixty feet have been reported. This fish has more than 100 rows of small teeth, but it only feeds on plankton and is harmless to humans. Swimming lazily in tropical seas, this shark doesn't seem to mind when people hitch a ride by holding its fins.

Q: DO SHARKS LOSE THEIR TEETH?

Answer: Yes, but they also replace them. Most sharks lose and replace their teeth many times. The great white shark, for example, has several rows of sharp, triangular teeth. Because the teeth are not securely set in the shark's jaws, often a tooth works loose or a worn tooth falls out. When a tooth in one row is lost, another tooth moves up from the row behind to take its place.

Q: DO ALL FISH HAVE SCALES?

Answer: No. Scales are thin, bony plates that grow in a protective layer on many fish, but not on all fish. Catfish, for example, do not have scales. Sharks, such as the small, spiny dogfish shark, do not have scales, either. Sharkskin is covered with tiny, rough "skin teeth" called denticles. The skin is so rough that many years ago cabinetmakers used sharkskin known as *shagreen* to sand and polish wood!

Q: DO FLYING FISH REALLY FLY?

Answer: Flying fish do not "fly" in the way that birds do. The flying fish is really a gliding fish. Although this sea creature spends most of its time in the water, it may take to the air to avoid an enemy. To "launch" itself, the fish swims rapidly up toward the surface. As its head leaves the water, the fish beats its tail to give itself an extra push. It then glides on its outspread fins for a distance of up to 650 feet, at a speed that may reach thirty-five miles an hour.

Q: WHAT ARE SPONGES?

Answer: Sponges are very simple animals that come in many shapes and sizes. They do not have muscles or nervous systems, but most have skeletons that give them shape and some protection. The body of a sponge is filled with tiny canals that allow seawater to move in and out. The animal filters its food directly from the water. There are about 5,000 different kinds of sponges, most of which live in colonies anchored to the sea bottom.

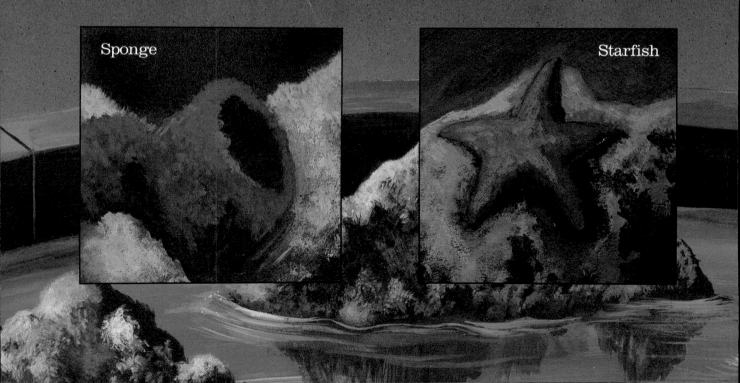

Sponge

Starfish

Q: ARE STARFISH REALLY FISH?

Answer: No. Starfish belong to a large family of animals called echinoderms (ee-KY-nuh-dermz). Other members of this family include sea urchins and sand dollars. Starfish come in a wide variety of sizes and colors. Most starfish have five arms and a unique star shape. The arms are lined with tiny tube feet that enable the starfish to move across the ocean floor. These tube feet also allow the starfish to cling securely to rocks, even in rough surf.

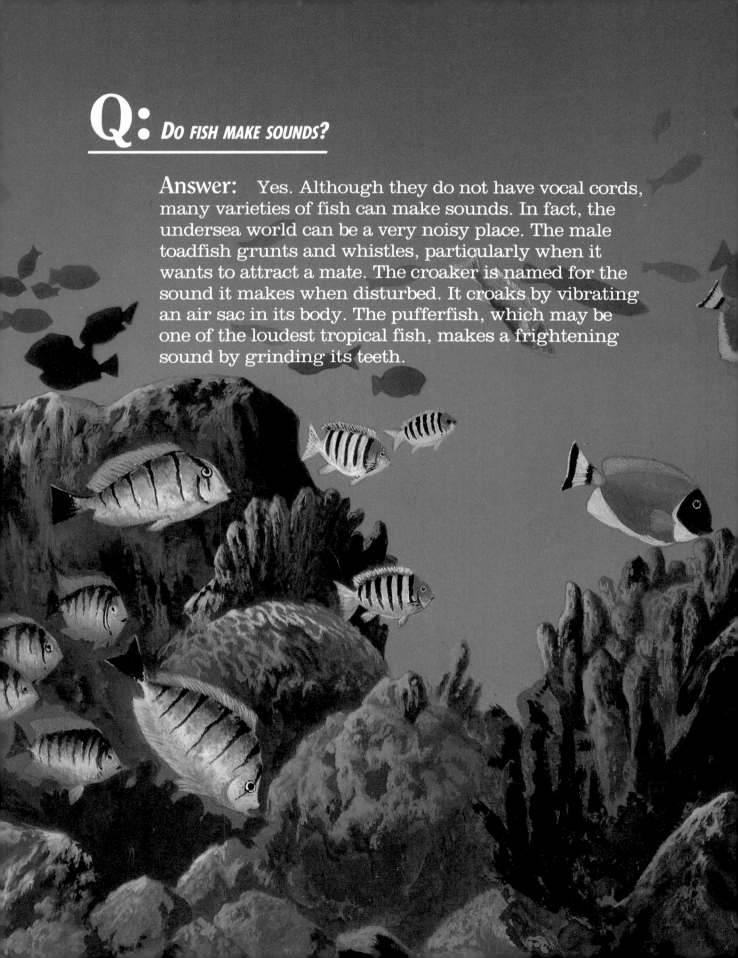

Q: DO FISH MAKE SOUNDS?

Answer: Yes. Although they do not have vocal cords, many varieties of fish can make sounds. In fact, the undersea world can be a very noisy place. The male toadfish grunts and whistles, particularly when it wants to attract a mate. The croaker is named for the sound it makes when disturbed. It croaks by vibrating an air sac in its body. The pufferfish, which may be one of the loudest tropical fish, makes a frightening sound by grinding its teeth.

Q: *HOW DO FISH BREATHE IN WATER?*

Answer: Fish breathe through special organs called gills. A fish usually takes water in through its mouth and pumps it over two sets of gills located behind and on either side of the mouth. The gills are filled with tiny blood vessels. At the gills, oxygen gathered from the water enters the animal's blood, and carbon dioxide leaves its system. The water flows out of the fish's body through openings on the sides of its head.

Q: HOW DEEP CAN HUMANS DIVE?

Answer: Without special equipment, most humans are restricted to about the first fifty feet or so below the ocean's surface. But people are fascinated by the underwater world and have developed ways to explore it. Equipped with scuba gear, divers can descend down to 120 feet beneath the surface. With special mixtures of breathable gas the limit is 500 feet, and divers wearing special protective suits can dive nearly 2,000 feet deep. In 1960, an underwater craft called the *Trieste* carried a human crew to the depths of the Marianas Trench, about 35,000 feet down.

Q: WHY IS THE OCEAN IMPORTANT TO HUMANS?

Answer: The ocean is important for a great many reasons. For example, life on Earth began in the ocean. Ocean waters help to moderate our climate. Tropical waters store heat and carry it to colder shores. The sea also gives us many kinds of foods to eat. To preserve and protect the ocean we must treat it with respect. We must keep it clean and protect all the living things that make it their home. The future of humankind has always been, and always will be, closely linked to the survival of the ocean.

Here are several other questions to consider about the ocean.

WHAT CAUSES OCEAN CURRENTS?

WHAT ARE HOT VENTS?

HOW DOES WATER REACH THE OCEAN?

HOW DOES A CORAL REEF FORM?

WHAT IS A WHIRLPOOL?

ARE ALL SHARKS DANGEROUS?

IS A DOLPHIN A FISH?

HAS ANYONE EVER SEEN A GIANT SQUID?

WHAT'S THE BIGGEST WHALE?

HOW DO WHALES AND DOLPHINS COMMUNICATE?

WHAT IS A JELLYFISH?

WILL PEOPLE EVER LIVE IN THE OCEAN?

These books will help you discover the answers:

Barle, Olive L.: *Strange Fishes of the Sea,* New York City, Morrow Junior Books, 1968.

Berrill, Jacqueline, and Berrill, N.J.: *1001 Questions Answered About the Seashore,* New York City, Dover Books, 1976.

Rockell, Bernard W.: *Whales and Dolphins,* New York City, Puffin Books, 1975.

Simon, Seymour: *Strange Creatures,* New York City, Four Winds Press, 1981.